Be *FUNNY...*
or *DIE!* :)

The *1-Night Stand* Quickie Guide that Will Make You Ridiculously **FUNNY**, *Even If You're Not*, like Your Life Depends On It...or *DIE!*

GABRIEL ANGELO

Copyright © SN & NS Publications, all rights reserved. It is impermissible to reproduce any part of this book without prior consent. All violations will be prosecuted to the fullest extent of the law.

While attempts have been made to verify the information contained within this publication, neither the author nor the publisher assumes any responsibility for errors, omissions, interpretation or usage of the subject matter herein.

This publication contains the opinions and ideas of its author and is intended for informational purpose only. The author and publisher shall in no even held liable for any loss or other damages incurred from the usage of this publication.

1 - Gabriel Angelo

Be FUNNY or DIE!

Be FUNNY or DIE!

Dedicated to all those who laugh at others' jokes...

And god bless whichever soul discovers a talking pink elephant.

Be FUNNY or DIE!

Be FUNNY or DIE!

An Unnecessary Disclaimer: Even though you can have a 1-night stand quickie with this guide, the truth of the nature is, mastering the art of being funny takes practice to develop a long-lasting loving relationship with humor itself. Now let's start dating...

Be FUNNY or DIE!

What's in the Goody Bag:

CHAPTER 1 - "Everybody Loves a Funny Man."
Why is Being Funny Important?..............................*11*
The Purpose of Humor in Everyday Life...................*13*
Survival Mechanism..*15*
The Power Of Humor..*20*

CHAPTER 2 - "Unearthing the Archaeological Funny Bone."
What is Being Funny?..*26*
The Art of Humor..*28*
History of Humor..*33*
The Psychology Behind Being Funny.....................*36*
The Laughter Factor..*38*

CHAPTER 3 - "Poor You...Why Can't You Be Funny?"
Why Aren't You Funny?..*41*
Causes of You Being Not Funny.............................*45*
Funny People Just Want to Have Fun......................*46*
Destroy these Funny Bunny Killers.........................*51*

CHAPTER 4 - *"What Sorcery is This?"*

Funny Recipes to Spice Up Your Conversation.........*55*
Exaggeration..*56*
Outrageousness..*61*
Self-Deprecation..*61*
Sarcasm...*63*
Element of Surprise...*64*
Hidden Truth...*66*

CHAPTER 5 - *"Are You Laughing at What I Said...or at Me?"*

Funny-Saying vs. Funny-Being..................................*70*
Be Funny NOT Just Say Something Funny...............*71*
Comedy Elements for Funny-Being for Funny-Sayings...*73*
Be Funny Without Words...*79*
Develop Your Own Funny Character........................*82*
Comical Characters Archetypes to Adapt..................*84*
Comedy Stereotypes to Absorb..................................*86*

CHAPTER 6 - *"Give Me the Punch Line!"*

The Art of Creative-Wit Humor.................................*90*

Bantering - The Art of the One-Liners......*91*
Spontaneity......*96*
Go With the Flow......*101*
Use Witty-Humor to Get Out of Sticky Situations......*102*
How to Tell Jokes......*105*
Create Your Own Jokes......*107*
WEEKLY CREATIVE-WIT TRAINING......*111*

CHAPTER 7 - *"Now I Got a Funny Story to Tell You..."*
Storytelling Comedy......*114*
The Art of Comical Storytelling......*116*
Create Your Funny Story......*122*

CHAPTER 8 - *"I Like You...You're Funny!"*
Apply Humor in Everyday Life......*130*
See the Funny in Everything......*131*
Train Your Brain Right......*134*
Gosh...You're Damn Funny as Hell! *Stop Making Me Laugh!* :D......*140*

Be FUNNY or DIE!

CHAPTER 1

"Everybody Loves a Funny Man."

Why is Being Funny Important?

As you now begin the journey of understanding how to be a **funny person**, most people will ask themselves this very important question, is it necessary to be funny? Especially for adults?

To answer this question, we are going to look at the benefits of being humorous and the sentimental value that accompanies being funny.

Not everyone is bound to be a funny person, but it is, however, very important to know when to step up to the plate and display the funny person in you. This is very important because in order to create social atmospheres where conversations can be enjoyed, humor must be an ingredient.

Conversations are important facets to human beings because they help people to understand each other further. Yet, most people tend to avoid conversations for the fear of being proselytized.

A funny person can, on the other hand, tactfully initiate a conversation, without the urge to change someone's opinion or without being judgmental at other peoples preferences.

It is therefore very important to learn how to be to be funny so that other people can open up to conversations with you, knowing that you do not wish to investigate their ideologies.

With this in mind, we cannot expect everyone be willing to pursue wanting to be more funny like a messianic complex. Unfortunately then, being a serious deadbeat makes less people want to associate with you because of the lack of feel-goodness that comes from being around funny people.

The Purpose of Humor in Everyday Life

Humor is considered to be a very powerful tool for human beings which helps us to accept and to be accepted by other human beings. Humor normally achieves this by lowering or eliminating the emotional barriers that are part of every individual's everyday life.

Through this mechanism, humor creates an effect, best described as an **attraction**, which thus opens the doors of acceptance between people. Hence, most of the time it does not matter how angry, sad or serious a person is, but when a witty statement or movements are made, it has the ability of lightening the current situation, suddenly uncovering a tension free atmosphere.

By doing this, a funny person makes the ease of establishing a close relationship with other people seem effortless. Being funny is therefore a very important part of human beings since it brings out the social nature of being human.

While going through the different stages in life, a person's social preferences begin to be shaped according to the different life experiences that one goes through. During this identity creation process, most people learn, especially through embarrassing situations, how to disguise and protect their emotions.

As we grow older and the demands of life increase, we completely forget the lively part that once existed in us. However, just like water nourishes a withered plant, so does humor awake the strangled child within us.

If you keenly look at people as they laugh, you will not fail to realize the joy brought out during the activity.

In our everyday lives, it can be noted that funny people always have the tendency to receive several privileges. However minimal, these privileges go a long way in explaining the importance of being funny. This includes things like being invited to events and other social functions.

Being funny also provides the privilege of solving conflicts easily and quickly, while avoiding the escalation of the same.

Nevertheless, being funny can be one rather complex task because of the discerning approach, perfect timing and perspicacious wit that funny people posses.

The ability to draw attention to a very huge *(sometimes sensitive)* topic within a small period of time and using minimal effort, requires not only talent but self-confidence and an incisive decision making process. This is because to become funny, you have to weigh situations, and chose the appropriate words, with the risk of being insensitive or offensive.

Survival Mechanism

It is also obvious that you have found *yourself* in situations whereby you laughed at a joke, but you did not understand any bit of the joke, let alone its relevance.

Basically, you laugh because every other person is laughing or you laugh to impress the other person. This comes most of the time when your superior, someone who intimidates you or someone with a high social status cracks a joke.

This raises an all important aspect of being humorous and being funny.

Is it a survival mechanism? Yes, it is.

Being funny is a **social survival mechanism.**

For most people, several challenges that they have in life has led them to hide under the cloak of humor so as to get through the societal challenges. These challenges include things like racism, being overweight or being too smart *(nerdy or geeky)*.

In order to be a funny person, you have to strike the *social imagination* of the people around you. Through this, you tackle three main categories of social imagination that you can use to derive jokes from:

- Superiority Theories

The first one is perfectly explained by the **Superiority Theories**. As a funny person, you can chose to derive jokes from a person whom seems to be lesser than you.

This kind of derisive humor normally target the inadequacies of other people, *for instance*, their accent, their walking style and any other misfortunes that might put you in vain glory over the other person.

- Incongruity Theories

The second category from which humor can be derived from is explained by the **Incongruity Theories**. These theories identify humor to arise from certain stereotypes that are formed against a certain group of people, but while telling the joke, you disappoint the audience by being incongruent with the normal perception.

A good example in this category is to assume that all Asians look alike or that lying is typical of a politician; but in the joke, you twist the expectation and make it sarcastic.

- Relief Theories

The third category from which you as a funny person can derive your humor is explained by the **Relief Theories**. Relief Theories suggest that you can become funny, by addressing the obvious indecencies in a comical manner. This fun type of humor is aimed at releasing the built-up nervous tension inside the muscles. This is why even offensive slurs can trigger humor. *In this theory*, you can make funny remarks, which are naturally abusive, but the people will find the humor embedded in it.

Examples in this category, include making abusive statements towards other cultural groups. The statements you make can be offensive, but due to the witticism applied, they become humorous, *for example*, racial or religious jokes.

***

As a social survival mechanism, you might find some things to be funny, just so that you can fit in. Most people also become funny because they express the internal fears that they harbor, which resonates well with other people who also have the same internal fears or similar experiences.

Through expressing your experiences with confidence and wit, you can turn that into your weapons of mass funniness.

The Power Of Humor

The effect that funny people bring to our otherwise hectic lives can be said to be *priceless*. The power of humor can thus be best described as *limitless*.

Below are some of the benefits that being funny can create among individuals or among groups of people:

- **Soothe Interactions and Solve Conflicts**

A funny person is always guaranteed to get along with other people. This is because the ability to initiate comfortable conversations ensures that you, *as a funny person*, does not step on other peoples' toes.

As a funny person, you are also gifted with the ability of being a good explainer; hence, able to solve conflicts easily through dialogue, before they escalate to bigger problems.

- **Bring People Together**

Ever heard of the phrase, *"Laugh, and the world will laugh with you"*? Well, the unifying aspect of laugher is undeniable. More often, you will find a group of people converged on listening to a funny story from a person.

The ability to unify people is brought about by the ability to be a good communicator; and a funny person is normally a good communicator, whom peoples' ears will always want to listen to for another extra minute. It is because of this that people who contain that same sense of humor will normally be more naturally bonded quite easily because of their shared so-called *"insider jokes"*.

By being a funny person, you are bound to bring people together.

- **Make People Like You**

Besides making people laugh, by being funny you are sure to be a very likeable person who make lasting impressions on people, enabling them to always remember you in a positive-light.

Just to slightly get off topic, this can be an important attribute especially to assist in learning. Students, scholars or any group of people who are trained by a funny person have the ability to effectively re-synthesize the concepts presented during the session. The reprocessing capability can be easily achieved if the learning was fun, or funny. Teachers and tutors who are funny are also likable their students.

By being a funny person, you are therefore more likely to be liked by your colleagues, employees, family members and other people who you associate with.

- **Get Further in Life and the Workplace**

Creative minds are normally said to be *funny minds*. This can not only be used to explain the development of animations, comics and cartoons, but also in development of simple business ideas.

Most of the time, simple and innovative ideas are formed as a result of previous funny experiences and future expectations. Through this creative thinking, a person with a humorous nature can develop important solutions; hence, advance in life, as well as within the workplace due to their humorous ways to be able to get along well with other people, earning him/her opportunities and other privileges. *(Just try cracking a joke with your boss and making him/her laugh.)* :)

This funny side can help anybody get further in life through the close relationship and bonds that are formed along the way at home or the workplace.

- **Have More Fun and Better Time, and Always Be Invited**

As it has been put out there before, laughter is indeed the *best medicine*. A funny person can be very helpful as a stress reliever.

As a social being, humans are expected to take frequent breaks when dealing with strenuous or emotionally draining activities and just have a good time. This is why people normally hang out and go out to have a good time and good laughs. By laughing regularly, a person is relieved of the stress which has been built up.

Being funny ensures that people always invite you out wanting to hang out because of the happy ambience that you bring along with you. Because of this, if you become a funny person will always be called back to events and invited to other new events.

***

Being funny ensures that you get the best of life. That is the ultimate goal of living, to have a better day than the previous one. It is for this reason that building your sense of humor is the best investment you can ever make.

CHAPTER 2

"Unearthing the Archaeological Funny Bone."

What is Being Funny?

Whereas every individual possesses a recognizably distinguishable sense of humor, there also exists other several categories of stimuli that precipitate humor in every person, ideally referred to as **universal stimuli**.

Different people have different senses of humor, *in that*, whatever you may consider to be a funny, hilarious or humorous statement or action, your friend or another person may find it just normal or, *even worse*, absurd.

Why do people vary in categorizing what they refer to as humor? Why does a fifteen year old find his teacher sliding on a banana peel funny, while you find it deadly serious?

When presented with a similar experience, what you consider funny and your friend doesn't, is actually based on the unique point of view that you two possess internally, best known as **perception**.

It is perfectly clear that being funny will always be dependent on the audience that you have. However, by understanding the universal stimuli that trigger humor, being funny can be approached on a broader perspective before narrowing it down to the exact people that you are targeting.

At this point you are probably asking, what are these universal stimuli that can be tapped into in order for to be perceived as being funny?

Well, there is no guarantee walking in a clown suit automatically makes you funny. However, there are some of the characteristics to be looked when comes to being funny.

These include; *pleasant surprises, startling experiences, ludicrous events, incongruity* and *tranquility*.

From identifying what being funny entails, you can authoritatively grasp how humor works. The inner-working of humor can be summed up as the mental ability to express or appreciate absurdity, pleasant surprises and incongruity.

With this in mind, the art of humor can now be focused on producing these stimuli which are considered to be the universal stimuli of humor.

The Art of Humor

Humor can also be classified as an **art**. Just like defining a talent, there lies a paradox in trying to explain what art is. Some people are born naturally humorous, while others work towards being humorous, like anything else you do in life. It is therefore important to note that as an art, humor contains its perfect imperfections like congruity.

The art of humor requires magnanimous skill and minimal strength in order to present it successfully. This is because of the sensitive nature of being funny, whereby *absurdity* is supposed to make people giggle or laugh and *verbal abuses* are supposed to be taken as jokes.

A simple mistake, especially in **timing**, and the whole aspect of trying to be humorous turns into a flop.

The art of humor for this reason demands that when you want to be funny, you have to identify your audience and perform a light research on the type of jokes to present to them. After that, it's now time to analyze the universal stimuli on which your humorous actions and talk will depend on:

- Incongruity

Incongruity can be best presented by using the art of speech or literature called an **oxymoron**. By being self-contradictory in a witty way, you present humorous statements by using paradoxes.

As a stimulus, a particular audience, *for example*, doctors would be enticed by incongruent statements that fit their carrier genre. A statement such as, *"the living dead"* would not be perceived too humorous by athletes, whereas physicians and medical practitioners would arguably tell the incongruence; hence, they can identify the humor.

Other incongruent phrases that you can use to deduce humor include: *"to act naturally," "a genuine imitation," "a working vacation,"* et cetera.

- Absurdity and Ludicrousness

You can also be able to express humor by using **absurdity** and **exaggeration**. This stirs an eccentric feeling, hence *"precipitating humor."*

This can also be achieved by the use of deliberate errors in your words. By mincing consonants and vowels in words, you can achieve the effect known as **spoonerism**.

- **Pleasant Surprises**

Humor can also be derived from the use of **pleasant surprises**. By exploiting this art, you would be required to spin *normal events* into much *unexpected happening*, especially as you're near the end of the event.

This technique is widely used by artists as the closing remarks in their presentations, commonly referred to as **punch lines**. However, surprises can also turn out to be shocking.

Startling experiences are known to create a build-up in adrenaline, but after discovering that the condition is not a threatening one, the person relaxes and the moment ends up to be humorous.

- Tranquility

You will find out that most of the thoughts and experiences that you have are shared by many other people.

Finding an opportune moment and the correct approach of explaining these shared experiences can turn out to be very humorous. This cognitive appreciation of the previous events is considered a stimulus for humor. However, you can also use previous *chaotic encounters* as stimuli for humor.

This is why sometimes when you are sited alone, and your memory jogs into a previous serious encounter, you can burst into laughter.

Remember as a young teenager when you and your friends would be chased by the homeless guy when it may not have been funny at that time?

History of Humor

The history of humor can be traced back to the biblical times of Solomon. Throughout man's life, comedians have always earned soft spots for powerful leaders. This is evident in the plays which were written by the authors dating back to 5th century BC.

As probably noted, the funny people, often referred to as **fools** had the privilege of making statements which were naturally derogatory, but they got away with it.

In *"The Merchant of Venice,"* William Shakespeare presented this fool as **Launcelot Gobbo**.

In the Greek and Roman Empire respectively, humor has served diverse purposes in their lives. However, a point to note that has been captured and that is being used up to date is the ability of using humor therapeutically.

In the Bible, the book of Proverbs, *Chapter 17 Verse 22* says that laughter is a good medicine for the heart, but lack of it is a disease. Now not saying that every person who uses humor as therapy reads the bible, but in ancient Greece, physicians would recommend their patients to visit entertainment theaters as part of their treatment.

Court jesters were also art of the administrative staff who aided the governors to relieve the stress that they accumulated while serving the citizens. This was necessary so as to enable the governors to provide quality service to the citizens.

Humor has evolved over different periods, and specific methods of presenting humor have been dominant during certain times.

In ancient Greece, some of these have been categorized into **Old Comedy** *(Archaia, 6th and 5th BC)*, **Middle Comedy** *(Mese, 5th and 4th BC)* and **New Comedy** *(Nea, 4th and 3rd BC)*.

Old Comedy is known to have focused on making political satires. It involved a lot of *personification* and *impersonation* of prominent political figures.

Unlike Old Comedy, Middle Comedy totally ignored impersonation, but focused on delivering *literal* and *social* comedy. Through this method, comedy was presented using the average citizens as the characters.

In the era of the New Comedy, the Athenian theatres in Greece were treated to comical presentations which involved *different characters* who were in their original form. Basically, these non-personified characters would go about their daily lives, but focus would be laid on their personal lives.

Some of the favorite names in early comedy include; Aristophanes, Menander, Dante Alighieri Giovanni Boccaccio, Geoffrey Chaucer, Erasmus, William Shakespeare among others.

The Psychology Behind Being Funny

As stated early, you do not necessarily have to be born naturally funny. You can become funny as you grow because of the various experiences that you go through or by being around a certain kind of people.

Let's look at the components of being funny. These include wit, mirth and laughter.

> **Wit** can be described as an aptitude for determining cleverly used facets in an event to fully understand an underlying meaning. Therefore, wit appreciates the intellectual light nature of complex things and assists you to change the perspective of things and look at them lightly and thus, wit is mental.

Mirth, on the other hand, is an emotional intuition that provokes feelings such as pleasure and joy which are basically associated with humor. Mirth is an involuntary and instinctive psychological occurrence that can happen even in the midst of a serious or sad situation.

Lastly, **laughter** is described as the physiological effect of humor. In full, humor is a complex process that involves wit *(mental)*, mirth *(emotions)* and laughter *(physiological)* responses.

By understanding these fundamentals of the psychology behind humor, you can identify the appropriate way of being funny. This can enable you to appreciate the humor when noticed in other people's actions or to be able to cause other people to appreciate our humorous gestures and actions.

In order to fully understand the importance of studying the psychology of humor, let's define the term *"psychology."* This is the study of a particular behavior, its causes and the consequences of the behavior.

In this case, humor **IS** the behavior. By analyzing humor psychologically, you will be able to identify where the humor is, predict when and under what conditions to best use it.

Through this, you can now be able to control it and apply it as and to an individual.

The Laughter Factor

In the end, **laughter** is a subconscious physiological response to humorous stimuli. Yet, you can easily choose to inhibit laughing out loud, but we cannot choose to stop its precipitation.

An interesting observation is that, it is not a *deliberate joke* that triggers laughter all the time.

Do you tell infants jokes in order for them to laugh? *Probably not.*

So the first reason as to why you laugh is...you were *born with laughter* in you. It is a genetic encoding among the various primates, including apes, as much as they do not laugh in the conventional human ways, they do produce facial expressions, body movements and sounds relatable to the way humans laugh.

Secondly, you laugh because it is *contagious*. Most of the time you might find yourself laughing, not because you have seen or heard a funny thing ,but because you have seen somebody else who is laughing.

As a human being, you might also choose to look for an environment where you will experience laughter. Such environments are normally *"feel good"* places when most of the time you are flanked by either close friends or family members, it is normal to want to relax and unwind after hectic events.

Finally, some people also laugh because of therapeutic reasons. In this case, the term *"laughter is the best medicine"* is applicable here.

CHAPTER 3

"Poor You...Why Can't You Be Funny?"

Why Aren't You Funny?

Does everybody wish they could be funnier? *Absolutely!*

Apparently, it is the wish of every individual to be a little bit funnier than they are at the moment...and includes you. You wish to be funnier than you are for that is why you are reading this now. Yet, this does not mean that every person who wants to be funnier is not funny.

Now being funnier or less funny has serious implications on your social life, and personal life too. *How is this so?*

Here are both the implications of you being more funny and the implications of you becoming less fun.

Being LESS Funny

By becoming **less funny,** you ought to be certain that your personal life and social life will go to the dogs. Let us look at a scenario in which you become less funny than you were before.

In this situation, you will lose a part of your thriving social life. This is because the people who normally hanged around with you will find you less interesting. You will find that they go to events without inviting you and doing your regular activities without giving you a heads up. That can be discouraging, a feeling only comparable to betrayal.

As for your personal relationships, they will also get a certain strain. Your partner or family will consider you to be more serious or less interesting. This normally takes a toll on your relationship, and it might escalate into deeper issues.

If not addressed openly, the stress and feeling of abandonment can have serious effects on your level and quality of productivity due to such psychological discomfort.

This, however, does not mean that you should go out of your way trying to prove that you can become funny again. The secret here is to make sure that you always maintain your sense of humor only when necessary. Trying too much can also mean irritating, or being out of context, and still lose the aura brought about by interesting people.

Being MORE Funny

In the second scenario, we are going to highlight the effects of becoming **more funny**. Does it work to your advantage? The answer is, *ALWAYS*.

Becoming more funny will always work to your own advantage, both socially and personally.

In a social context, becoming more funny means that you will get to acquire more friends and make new connections.

The eccentric atmosphere that you carry around with you as a person also means that your stress hormones are always kept on a low. As a result, becoming more funny increases the likelihood of you being more productive in everything that you do, from your career, your personal relationships into your social life.

Becoming more funny will also earn you more privileges and favors big or small, as we witnessed in the *previous chapter*.

With this in mind, it is, without a doubt, inevitable for anyone, including you, to learn to become more funny. We have witnessed more funny people in real life, always having interesting times.

Who would not want to have a exciting life and feel appreciated by other people?

Causes of You Being Not Funny

Now why can't you be funny?

This question does not come as a surprise to many. Yet, it is still surprising that you cannot be funny, and it is not just you.

Better question should be *"What makes you not to be funny?"*

Nevertheless, have you ever said something that made everyone burst into laughter, while ideally you never intended to crack a joke?

Yes, if we can go back into time and tap into that moment, we would identify all the necessary ingredients that made you funny at that exact moment.

However, since we are here to understand how to become more funny, let us look at the things that make us **less fun** because being *"funny"* and *"fun"* go hand and hand and are connected.

The more funny you are, the more fun you have; and the more fun you have, the more funny you can be.

This way, have fun to be funny. You get the best of both worlds. *Duh!*

Funny People Just Want to Have Fun

An important disclaimer first; the things that make you less fun do not necessarily mean that they are negative traits in life. Self-composure and personally remaining principled has their own advantages in most other important aspects of life.

Below are some of the traits that make you not fun and funny:

- **Turning Down Proposed Fun Activities**

It can get very irksome if you are around people who are not down for the activities that will make you have the time of your life. These people shoot down every attempt and suggestion that you make about having fun. This is a person who never wants to try anything new or even worse, this person never wants to try anything; or if they do, they want to quit halfway.

Heck, the person being described might be you. This makes you not fun to be with, hence not funny.

- **Holding Back Too Much**

One common character about non-fun people is that they always hold back too much.

If for example there is an office party, you are not supposed to sit pretty and wait to be approached by your fellow employees. You become less funny when you do not interact with others; yet be sure that you maintain your composure also by not going overboard.

Do not be that person who is sited at the corner by *himself* or *herself* staring out of the window into the sky, at a party. If you don't move around to loosen up and chat up your co-workers in a staff party, then this is why you are **not funny**.

Relax. Have a drink.

You do not need to be the one creating the fun, but by positively participating in the ongoing activities, the funny person inside you will just show outward.

- **Being Too Meticulous**

Paying so much attention to detail is another way of being less funny. Thoughts like *"I would have talked to them, but they are not my type"* or *"this place would be more exciting if they played my type of music"* are a serious buzz killer.

You cannot be funny if you do not get out of your comfort zone. Of course this does not necessarily mean that you should go on trying and doing everything that comes your way. The standards of the people or the standards of the environment might be lower, according to your likeness, but this should not hinder you from participating in the fun.

Imagine going to a hiking adventure and you start wishing that the roads would be perfect. *Oh please*, you are already killing the fun in hiking by even thinking like that.

If you are normally being too meticulous, that is another reason why you are not funny.

- **You Are a Downer**

Just let funny moments be funny moments while it lasts. This is another reason that makes you unfunny.

You can imagine the moment when you are kicking it with your pals, just having a good time, than one of your friends' starts to complain over every little detail. This nagging is a total buzz kill.

Another way of becoming a downer is by introducing uncomfortable moments and depressing topics while people are trying to have a good time.

Fact of matter is, nobody likes to be around such a person when they want to have fun. *And guess what?* Next time you will not be invited. **Period.**

- **You Are So Serious All the Time**

Have you ever seen a CEO of a multimillion dollar company discussing the company's financial reports? Or if you are a CEO, imagine that board meeting where you review the sales trends of your company's product for the past 3 months.

That kind of seriousness should always be left for serious matters.

When you go on a night out, repeat this oath: "*Thou shall* not get offended by the drunkards. *Thou shall* not get embarrassed by how folks dance. *Thou shall* not maintain the conversational tone and topics like the one left at seriously for work."

Loosen up when the time calls for it, this way you will not be the least funny person.

Having fun and being funny all have to do with lowering your **seriousness shield** and appreciating some controlled wild immature thoughts and actions. Now this does not mean that you are becoming baseless, puerile, shallow or vacuous. Far from that.

If anything else, by loosening up, will make you adapt to different situations easily.

Destroy these Funny Bunny Killers

We have just talked about the things that you can do in order to avoid being not fun and funny.

Now we will look at the characteristic traits that make you not funny, like an unfunny bunny caught in a cage.

This section and the previous one might sound almost the same, but as you go through this, you will clearly understand the difference.

- Lacking Sense of Humor

The first one is the lack of sense of humor. In this case, the lack of a sense of humor makes you rigid and serious about everything.

Lacking a sense of humor means that everything you look at or hear will be categorized only through one lens, just the way it is. This means that you can't even laugh at yourself or at others.

- Being Overly Logical

Secondly, being logical in all situations kills humor adversely. In some situation, you need to avoid being logical in order to bring out the humor in the situation.

The best example where logic should be avoided is in fictional stories. If you dismiss the possibility of a flying man, then Superman or Spiderman will never be appreciated; and your jokes will not be funny disabling your creative mind. Logic kills humor.

- Being Easily Offended

Lastly, if you are offended emotionally very easily, then you can never be funny. Being funny means being able to take jokes lightly and not harboring them as personal jibes. This enables you to take jokes as jokes and not to perceive them out of context.

If you get offended easily, then people will bypass you because no one would want to offend you through a joke. For instance, it is also normal that pranks are played amongst friends, colleagues and families, thus, if such prank cannot be played on you because you might take it personally, then the joke is on you. A prank, after all, is only supposed to be an amusing joke for good old fun and a good laugh.

***

At the end of it all, the goal of this chapter is to bring out the required personal traits that are associated with being funny.

By going back over what's discussed above, you can be sure that your sense of humor and propensity to fun will definitely change for the better.

CHAPTER 4

"What Sorcery is This?"

Funny Recipes to Spice Up Your Conversation

Your interaction with other people will always provide the final attribute of your personality. But to really portray yourself as a likeable and funny person, you really to spice up the charm with your conversation being a killer.

Surely you have been in a situation where you thought someone was a jerk, until you went and talked to them; or you thought someone was boring, until you spent some time with them.

In this chapter, you will be introduced to the most basic ingredients in which you use to can spice up your conversations to be more interestingly funny: *Exaggeration, Outrageousness, Self-Deprecation, Sarcasm, Hidden Truths,* and through the *Element of Surprise.*

Exaggeration

Most people keep you interested in their conversations and actions because they *exaggerate.*

Exaggeration is the art of amplifying or diminishing the actual proportions of a statement, event, or object. This is a fun way of creating humor during a conversation, and it is a sure darn way of keeping things interesting.

In artistic presentations, caricatures are used by the artist to achieve aggrandizement of some features of a popular or normal character, while still leaving hints of identifying or recognizing the real person. This always works and it normally brings out the intended humor.

I am sure you have seen either sculptures or drawings of a popular politician and they always crack you up.

The only way of using exaggeration in a perfect manner is by inflating or deflating the **facts** of whatever you are conversing about so much in a manner that they obviously look like either an *understatement* or an *overstatement*.

So how do you effectively use exaggeration, in other words, how do you make a big deal out of nothing and still maintain the humor?

- **Identify a Unique or Pronounced Feature**

Every conversation has a topic, and every topic involves a subject which is either an *object* or a *person*. When discussing about a certain topic, the subject of the topic is bound to contain either a **deficiency** or a **pronounced feature.**

In order to use exaggeration effectively, this pronounced or unique feature will help you to propagate your intentions.

A good example is when talking about your neighbors' short husband. The fact that your neighbors' husband is already short, and that it is noticeable, go further to describe the shortness of that person. So in essence, this is how you will present the subject.

"My neighbors' husband is soo short that...when discussing an awesome event, you should stress the fact the event was so awesome that..."

- **Setup a Relationship Between the Feature and another Extreme Feature**

The essence of exaggeration is to *portray* an **extreme image.** This can be achieved by comparing two features on either side of the extreme. Let us build up on my neighbors' short husband. We will make a link between him being short and attach it to another extremely short or extremely little object or person. So it will go like this:

"My neighbors' husband is 300ml short of a can of his favorite soda."

We all know how small a 300ml can looks like. Comparing my neighbors' husband shortness with the size of a can, portrays an extreme exaggeration that can only be described as insane.

Alternatively, we can use an extremely bigger subject to portray exaggeration and achieve the same effect.

For example, you should know how tall basketball star Shaquille O'Neil is. If you don't, here is a brief description of his physique: he is 7 ft 1 in tall *(that is approximately 2.16m)* and weighs about 325 lbs *(which is approximately 148kg)*. By now, you get the point. Don't you?

- **Deliver the Punch Line**

At this point in your conversation, you have already built the anxiety that can only be best described as a **ripened anxiety**. The most important thing is to deliver the punch line that would leave your listener or audience on the floor laughing their ribs out.

Without keeping you waiting any longer with the suspense, let's go straight to deliver the punch line of the conversation that was built up earlier, with the neighbors' short husband as the subject.

"My neighbors' husband is so short that a 300ml can of his favorite soda…blocks his view on the street."

Now that's funny, but alternatively.

"My neighbors' husband is so short that on his birthday, Shaquille O'Neil brought him a feeding bottle."

Outrageousness

Being **outrageous** and **crazy** require adequate self-confidence and a free spirit; however, too much craziness can be a turn-off. You should always know the appropriate moment to display your outrageousness.

For example, you cannot just decide to throw a tantrum in a board meeting when very serious discussions are undergoing. On the other hand, when you are just leaving the office at the end of the week, you can yell, *"THANK GOD IT'S FRIDAY!"*

You will get away with being crazy in this situation.

Self-Deprecation

Self-deprecation is defined as the act of negatively blowing your own trumpet. This is a bold way of accepting your own flaws to a level that you can even make jokes about yourself.

Typical self-deprecating jokes that can be used to spice up conversations, include joking about your race, joking about your body weight or joking about your love life.

An example of a self-deprecating joke about a person's love life goes like this:

Do you know the feeling you get when you meet a person and both of you just fall madly in love with each other? Yeah... me neither."

Another example of a self-deprecating joke is about body weight, whereby a person acknowledges that they are in shape while they are not, like for example:

"I believe I am in awesome awesome shape, but round is also a shape, right?"

Sarcasm

Sarcasm, the epitome of *wit* that makes a point of portraying the opposite of the intended reaction.

Sarcasm is to said to be a developed form of humor that requires a *social understanding* between the different parties in a conversation. Sadly, or interestingly, enough, sarcasm always comes out as an advice or a suggestion that is always positively negative. *(If it makes any sense.)*

And true to the origin of the word sarcasm, it means a "mean feat," derived from an ancient Greek word *"sarkasmos,"* which stands for *"tearing flesh, gnashing the teeth, or speaking bitterly."* On its own definition, sarcasm is defined as *"a bitter sharp, cutting remark or a bitter taunt or gibe."* However, despite its harsh definitions, being sarcastic can, and is used to make fun in conversations.

The fact that sarcasm is always uttered with some contempt and bile, it can be a very sensitive way with which you can use to spice up your conversations. The basic threshold of using sarcasm is to ensure that whoever you use it with is a person whom you have a perfect understanding of.

Sarcasm can also be used by strangers, but it is important to do an external analysis of the person, and if they exhibit the signs of being able to positively take sarcasm, then you have a green light. This might also turn sour, but a sarcastic person will always pretend to be hurt by your remarks, and they counter your joke with another joke or sarcastic remark. So unless it happens that way, consider your sarcasm game treacherous.

Element of Surprise

The unexpected of humor in conversations can be a great asset to spicing your conversations. Every other time, people will be keen to listen to you with the expectation that something funny is going to come up with your conversation with them.

This can only be achieved by applying the **element of surprise** in your conversations. The unexpected surprise is a great way of twisting your conversations and delivering a pleasant ending.

To achieve this, you must learn to build the anticipation and enhance the surprise by acting normal in your conversation, until when it nears the end. You cannot build surprises in a conversation by starting with the joke because while building this anticipation, you might disappoint your audience by delivering a flat joke prematurely. That is why you act normal at in the first place. Do not look excited. This way, you can always pretend that you were not prepared for the interesting punch line.

The most effective way of applying the element of surprise is by ensuring that you apply "**the rule of three.**" The rule of three in comedy anticipates that as a comedian, you should *prepare your audience* with **two sets of illustration,** but *deliver a punch line* on the **third time.** The rule of three basically states that a conversation can be broken down into an introduction, the body and then the conclusion. This is a great tool that can be effective in spicing up your conversation to make them humorous and exciting.

For being funny in the rule of three, the third one should be the unanticipated not like the first two's:

"You should marry me because I'm rich, good-looking, and a mama's boy."

Hidden Truth

Humor can be utilized effectively to address **hidden truths.** In other words, you can spice up a conversation by humorously addressing the hidden blunt truths that everyone else seems to avoid.

The elephant in the room is normally an obvious cause of tension that needs careful reproach, because addressing it can be perceived as betrayal, rebellion or disrespect. Such conversations can be spiced up by tactfully accompanying the issue with a light statement.

An example of a hidden truth can be is normally displayed by the phrase *"just kidding."* There is always a truth in the statement that is accompanied by a *"just kidding."* This is because of the hostile nature of jokes, since they are mostly derived from people's imperfections.

Supposed you are a guy. Picture a scenario where a fat lady is trying to fit in a dress, and she turns and asks you, *"Does this dress make me look fat?"*

In such a case, what would a man do? What would you do? Well, the most comforting answer will not be, *"Yes, it makes you look fat."* It will be something like, *"Not really, although it looks a little bit tighter on the waist, but the rest is fine."*

***

From these **six above funny recipes** *(exaggeration, outrageousness, self-deprecation, sarcasm, hidden truths, and the element of surprise)*, you can now be assured that your conversations from now on will be spiced up to be interestingly funny.

The art of being an interesting speaker or an interesting listener can be worked on with the correct tools like the ones mentioned above.

Sprinkle them into your conversation, and always ensure that you have a brief knowledge about current events ranging from sports, politics, technology and even the newest television show in town.

Having brief knowledge in all these fields is just pre-heating the oven. You never know who's the next person you meet will be interested in.

CHAPTER 5

"Are You Laughing at What I Said...or at Me?"
Funny-Saying vs. Funny-Being

"Do I look funny to you?" – **Joe Pesci**, Goodfellas

Something is funny, because it captures a moment, like a Polaroid Hallmark moment. Saying something funny is so, because they are said in the right context, at that perfect time and to that correct crowd.

The way you <u>deliver</u> the words is hugely important too; your *tone of voice*, your *facial expression* and even your *body language* contributes to the end message.

The real question is...can you say something funny, without being a funny person?

Definitely, after all actors do it every single day of their lives. There are many comedy television or film stars who are actually very serious in real life. *(We're talking serious dead-beats.)*

So how do they manage to pull this off and get laughs...and more importantly, how can you do the same?

Be Funny NOT Just Say Something Funny

Popular funny sayings include:

"I'm not clumsy! The floor just hates me, the tables and chairs are bullies and the walls get in the way!"

Or

"I'm on a seafood diet. I see food, I eat it."

Now of course, as with all comedy, the humor within these phrases is subjective. Everybody finds different things funny.

However, try saying these things - out loud or in your mind - in a flat, boring tone of voice. With no emotion, there isn't even the slightest chance of anyone else picking up on the intended comedy.

Now try saying it again, this time really thinking about how you want the listener to hear the message; put emphasis where it's required, smile as you speak and gesture as appropriate.

It's already much more captivating isn't it?

Putting personality into the words, is going to make your audience, or whoever you are speaking to, pay more attention, and feel what you are trying to get across. Hence, you are more likely to get a laugh.

There are many ways to involve your personality, and things to involve into your personality for *"funny-being"* to produce *"funny-sayings."*

Comedy Elements for Funny-Being for Funny-Sayings

First, let's look at comedy elements:

- **Parody**

A **parody** is where you imitate the work of someone else, *for comedic effect*, and this can include using a funny saying often linked to a specific comedian, actor or other person.

For example, *"Nice to see you, to see you nice!"* is a very famous comedic quote from Bruce Forsyth which was always stated at the beginning of his television show. When other people use this saying, the audience immediately knows what they're referring and the familiarity of this makes them laugh.

This type of comedy has been used for many years; in fact it is cited by Aristotle to have been invented by Hegemon of Thasos by slightly altering the wording in well-known poetry - *all for comedic effect.*

For something that has worked for so many centuries, surely you should give it a go ahead fellow solider!

- Satire

People, who use **satire comedy,** mock a section of society or politics.

Now this type of humor can be very effective because everyone has an opinion of some sort when it comes to the way their country is run. *(Just be careful not to offend or alienate people!)*

Satire has been used in literature for a very long time, to demonstrate foolishness or vice in humans. These days, it is often seen in newspaper cartoons, which give a funny scope on the daily stories.

You can incorporate this into your own personality by taking something from current events/news and starting with a point of social commentary...something you, and your audience, want to change, and create a joke based on how little is being done to do this, *e.g.*, government changes.

Catch-22 is a satire of war, and a good place to start your research if you feel like this is something you'd like to try.

- Irony

This is based on the **opposite of expectation**. It can be an unexpected event occurring, or someone saying the opposite of what they mean. The lack of harmony between what *is happening*, and what the audience *thought would happen*, is where the humor lies.

An example of this might be meeting a very large dog, so huge that people will comment on it. However, the dog is named *"Tiny."* People will find this humorous, because they would not have thought to give such a large dog that name themselves.

Another way irony can be used with your personality, is by combining it with **slapstick** *(more on slapstick below)*.

For example, your friend may step in a muddle puddle, causing you to laugh. As you chuckle and mock them for their error, a car drives past covering you head to toe in mud. Of course, your friend will end up with the last laugh! *(Slapped back rite at ya!)*

Comedians often do use irony to point out societies errors, effectively combining it with **satire**.

For instance, it could be pointed out that a man left his job as a hugely important bank manager, to work as a road sweeper...and now they earn more darn money!

- Sarcasm

We've already gone over **sarcasm** previously on the different recipes to spice up your conversation.

Now using *sarcastic comments* with your personality to produce funny-sayings are often quick-fire, and said with the intention to point out an error, mistake or something silly. This works best as a response to an initial comment given by someone else, so frequently requires you to be able to think on your feet.

However, there are examples of where the statements can work in an isolated environment. Here are a couple of examples:

"I need something that only you can provide…your absence!"

Or.

"If you find it hard to laugh at yourself, I'm happy to do it for you!"

And.

"Marriage is the main cause of divorce."

Timing is important to make these comments funny, but if you manage to achieve that, sarcastic remarks often result in a laugh.

Just be careful not to mock someone so much that you hurt their feelings. This will negate the intended message, and turn your audience against you.

- Black Comedy

This is where a comedian will *add humor* to a very **dark** or **serious subject matter,** to try and bring light to it.

Sometimes it's possible to juxtapose the sadness with comedy to cause the audience to laugh.

An example of a black comedy joke would be:

Q: *"How do you stop a lawyer from drowning?"*

A: *"Shoot him before he hits the water."*

The subject of death is a serious and sad one, but the humor of this joke lies within the fact that many people have had a bad experience with a lawyer - they are known for overcharging for their services, and have a cold-hearted reputation.

Most people will laugh at this style of joke, *but again*, try not to offend or upset.

Be Funny Without Words

Now, we have looked at different comedy elements to involve into your personality to say funny things, but is it possible to be funny WITHOUT constantly having to make jokes and use funny-sayings?

There are many techniques that comedian's use that don't involve any usage of their words *(TRUE funny-being)*; but the humor is derived from their behaviors and actions not the actual words, and you can adapt some of these to your own self.

- Slapstick

This is all about silly, over the top funny physical events happening. It certainly doesn't need a funny-saying included to make the audience laugh.

It was often used to lighten the atmosphere in Shakespeare's plays in the form of chase scenes and beatings - *mock violence* is often a key factor in slapstick routines.

An example of a slapstick routine can be:

Man-A picks up a large plank of wood.

Man-B shouts, "Be careful with that!"

Man-A replies "Pardon?" whilst turning around and smacking Man-B around the face with the wood, knocking him to the ground. (poor fellow)

The comedy lies in the **ridiculous accident**, the exaggerated hurt and the way that the second man tried to prevent the entire incident...effectively setting it in motion.

- Spoof

There has been a trend in Hollywood, for spoof movies - mocking the stereotypes included in other films.

For example, a serial killer wearing a mask is a common scene in horror films. **Spoof imitations** will *have the mask fall off* early on, immediately revealing the killers face, ruining the mystery.

The key to making this type of humor work is ensuring that your audience knows exactly what you are mocking, so you will need to be sure that it is something they're familiar with.

Being forced to explain it will ruin the comedy effect.

- Farce

This type of comedy is caused by "**exaggerated characters**" in "**ridiculous situations**," which spiral rapidly, becoming more and more out of control. The purpose of this is pure entertainment, and often incorporates all the other types of comedy to assist in its humor.

You can use this yourself in the stories or jokes you tell, or in **the action you play**, if this is something you'd like to try.

Develop Your Own Funny Character

Be FUNNY or DIE!

Of course, anyone can tell jokes; they are simply a few words put together in a sentence. But not everyone can gain a laugh from these words.

You need to **portray your own character** within your words to get your audience's attention and to help them relate to you.

Few things to consider to develop your natural inner funny character.

- **Body language** and **facial expressions** are important.

- You need to come across as warm and inviting, to make people like you before you start on the humor, particularly if you're going to use **sarcasm** - you want to *avoid it being mistaken* for **insults**.

- You also need to be in tune to the **particular moment**. If your audience is in a bad mood, or doesn't seem interested, your joke will not work.

- You also need to think about the **timing** of your words. You need to build up **tension** as you speak and deliver the punch line at the exact timing.

This can be a learning curve, so gauge reaction as you go and tweak your performance accordingly.

Take ideas and inspiration from real people in your life and characters from movies to what you find funny and make you laugh, spinning them into your our character.

Comical Characters Archetypes to Adapt

There are many comical characters from stories that you can use for research or reference when developing your own character. They each provide humor in their own special way, something that you will need to do too.

- **The Jester** - This character in inherently silly. Every single thing they do is for the sole purpose of humor.

- **The Rebel** - This could be the anti-hero, the enemy or someone who works in an unorthodox manner alongside the 'good side'.

- **The Action Hero** - The hero is often over the top in strength and ability. Applying parody or slapstick to this will get a laugh from your audience.

- **The Intellect** - This character is generally very absent minded, but also brilliantly intelligent. The humor often comes from their ingenious inventions going wrong.

- **The Bimbo** - Female characters are often portrayed as dumb, simplistic and in need of rescue, "Damsel in Distress." Their manner is often farcical in nature.

Of course, there are many other characters and archetypes – after all every character provides a different sort of laugh for particular reason - but for the purposes of comedy, these are good places to start.

Comedy Stereotypes to Absorb

Comedy is also filled with "real life" stereotypes. They are very useful, because the audience can instantly make a connection and recognize the character without more of an explanation needed.

It has been done for a very long time as an effective medium of communication, and as long as it's done in a humorous, and not offensive way, it can cause a lot of laughs.

Examples of stereotypes include:

- **Nerd** - This character is clever, constantly speaking in complicated jargon, but with a distinct lack of social skills. They are often saying the wrong thing and awkward times.

- **Drug Dealer** - This person will have a tough exterior and a rough reputation. Concerned primarily with money and their clients, they are uncaring.

- **Gangster** - Another character obsessed with money and power. Gangster stereotypes are often played with an exaggerated Italian accent and a white cat.

- **Surfer** - Surfers are often shown as dumb, but fit men, obsessed only with the waves and finding the next great beach to try out.

- **Pothead** - A character who is always stoned will be red-eyed, lazy, constantly eating and saying things that they think are profound, but are actually stupid.

- **Goth** - A gothic character will always wear black and be covered in piercings and tattoos. They will be shown to hate everything, be constantly miserable and write depressing poetry.

This list is by no means extensive, there are many stereotypes you can include in your personal character - depending on what you like, what your audience thinks is funny and what the situation requires.

You can adapt these to your own personality and use them in a light-hearted way to cause your audience to laugh.

Combine these characters with the funny-sayings or actions and you are on your way to being a walking fireball of ridiculous funny-being of epic proportion.

CHAPTER 6

"Give Me the Punch Line!"

The Art of Creative-Wit Humor

WIT! WIT! WIT! Nuff said! This is the true core to be a walking, sexy funny machine *(and not the other way around)*.

The most prominent gift we all envied from a person with strong wit, who gets labeled as very funny, is the ability to think on their feet, be spontaneous and randomly pull out funny witty one-liners out of thin air that make us all laugh.

That is a technique called **bantering**.

Bantering - The Art of the One-Liners

According to the definition of Oxford Dictionary, *"banter"* is a friendly and playful exchange of teasing remarks. The keywords to be noted in this definition are the words "playful" and "teasing."

For a banter to be successful, it has to be quick, playful (witty) and teasing. Wit, as we have defined it earlier is considered as mental keenness that exudes pure intelligence.

Bantering requires lots of wit as it is considered as a quick exchange of teasing short remarks that feed off the previous remarks, almost instantly. That is why it is considered as the art of one-liners.

However, the use of banter requires some intellectual relationship. These relationships might include long term friendship, same carriers or same hobbies.

Below, is a list of ways in which you can improve your art of banter:

- **Be a keen listener**

First off, being an **avid listener** is the most important part of having a good conversation, and since banter is a conversation with quick short replies, being a good listener is inevitable.

In order to give a satisfactory remark to whatever the other person is saying, you have to fully understand what it they are saying in the first place is. From that, you can build on it and perfectly give a quite impressive answer that stands as relevant. This is also important because the person will get that you are on the same page with them.

To effectively apply this skill in banter, you can fully understand a person's remark and while offering your remark in exchange, you give a comparison that both of you can relate to.

- **Exaggeration**

You remember learning about the recipes to spice up conversation in Chapter 4?

By using **exaggeration** in banter, you can be assured of taking the conversation to another level. You will shift from one topic to another while elevating the humor in your conversation.

For example, when talking about running so fast, you can include, *"I ran so fast Usain Bolt wouldn't catch me if he tried."*

- **Pun Intended**

Intentional usage of **puns** can also be a great way of ensuring a successful banter.

In order to be more successful in your pun intentions, be *symbiotic*. Feed of the previous remarks of made by the other person. Use the words that they have used and apply it in a different context while still contributing to the ongoing conversation.

However, in banter, puns intended are supposed to remain within the genre/context of the current conversation in order to retain the wittiness in banter. *If not*, it will throw the conversation off-course, dealing a heavy blow to your banter.

An example of a pun is when you are talking about extraordinary animals, like your friend who doesn't eat processed pork, let's call him *"Hamfree,"* takes you to see a camel without a hump. They should also name the camel *"Humphrey."*

- **Be Metaphorical**

Suppose you are with your friend, and he tells you that he would like to take a trip to the moon, would you tell him to *"Beat it"*?

Well if you would tell him that, then your friend should be able to tell you, *"Thank you Michael Jackson, you're such a thriller."*

Now that's banter because it is short, quick, witty, pun intended and metaphoric at the same time.

The use of **metaphors** in banter comes in a somewhat sarcastic manner, although it does not have to be sarcastic. Metaphors are used as a graphical way of connecting a statement to a known fact.

Another example of a metaphor is a person who is fond of wearing watches, could that be big Ben?

- **Use Quotes from Famous Speakers, Movies, Books or Songs**

The reason why bantering requires a form of relationship, is because of the need for both parties to be *"in-on the joke."* Without familiarity of the statement, banter will pass as a statement not connected to the conversation, making you to look weird, when in fact you are just having an advanced sense of humor.

By using **quotes** in banter, both of you need to know the source of the quote for it to remain relevant, otherwise you will be forced to explain the quote, this kills the banter.

In a situation when your friend asks you, *"Are you afraid?"* You can interject and say, *"Everyone dies, whether today or fifty years from now."* Of course that is a quote from the movie, TROY, but unless both you and they know about it, it would not appear to be like a quote.

Spontaneity

It is quite oxymoronic that we can study *how to be spontaneous*. However, **spontaneity** is a necessary ingredient that spices up witty-humor.

Spontaneous humor has a refreshing effect on your conversation and it shows "*ay*" to connect with an audience. An impromptu comment will always portray your flexible sense of humor.

To be fully effective in spontaneous humor, you have to poses vast general knowledge, self-confidence and wit. You don't want to be blank when a question is thrown your way.

However, the following methods also can also help to improve your spontaneity.

- **Preparedness**

You can actually prepare to be spontaneous. This can be done by equipping yourself with words that you will say in certain situation. To the audience, they may appear as spontaneous, but in actual sense you were prepared for it.

Preparing for spontaneity might involve doing a background research on your audience, be it a person or a group. This will help you to understand their interests and the kind of things that would make them unhappy. Of course you will steer clear the things that annoy them.

- Observation

A keen person will notice obvious things, just like any other person, but due to their keenness, they will find exceptional things worth noting. This is the power of **observation.**

However, after making the observation, you create further humor by associating the *distinctive feature* with an *obvious feature* and paint out the unseen image that will resonate with your audience.

For example, when walking into an office, you can notice something quire, and to jump start the conversation, you can start by saying, *"While I was walking into your office I noticed..."*

- Self-Confidence

After preparation and observation, it is normally time to meet your audience. This is the point where that negative *"inner voice"* normally plays tricks on your courage. Several ideas pop in your mind but *alas*, there goes the inner voice, *"Don't say that."*

While this voice is playing tricks on your mind, the brain becomes disoriented, and either you just stand there looking like a fool, or you totally lose control of your composure. However, go with your *gut feeling*.

Intuition could ensure that you deliver great spontaneity. If it seems funny in your head, it probably is funny *(although not always)*.

But the point is, become bold and your spontaneity will appear by itself, or you will not lose focus of what you had prepared. Take a deep breath before starting a conversation and ensure that you are comfortable by yourself.

Another way to boost your confidence is to always ensure that you are well decently dressed according to the setting, well groomed and clean breath. *Yes that's also very important.*

- **Practice**

Practice makes perfect. Yes, it's a cliché, but it's so true. Spontaneity is a muscle, but most of the time we're so caught up in our usual restricted routine, that hampers our inclination to be spontaneous. By practicing your spontaneity, you get to exercise our observational techniques and your self-confidence.

For example, you can volunteer to talk in group activities and use this platform for making comments, observed during the meeting and other humorous things that you might be having in store. You can also practice in front of a mirror and other groups of people like family or your favorite vendors.

However, the greatest thing that can help you practice become spontaneous is getting involved in *improv* and *acting* aka **improvisational acting**. Join a local improv group and you'll start taking that skill from the theater into the real world, worthy of the Academy Award.

<u>Go With the Flow</u>

"Going with the flow" is synonymous with being **flexible**.

In order to effectively apply witty-humor, you have to be ready to switch from topic to topic comfortably.

This is also a basic rule of life, as there is no promise of a structured way of things happening. It also means that at times you have to get off your comfort zone.

Now, therefore, let's reiterate the importance of having bits of both *current* and *historical* knowledge in general topics across various fields.

In order to effectively go with the flow, there are some basic characteristics that you must possess. They include:

- Anticipating a shift in topics of discussion.

- Maintaining composure when discussions shift into areas where you are less familiar with.

- Have your facts, and discuss from the facts you have.

- Laugh and try to steer your conversation back to your area of comfort.

Use Witty-Humor to Get Out of Sticky Situations

Sticky situations are **serious business** to be monkeying around, *man*. Such kinds of situations if handled wrongly can mean a great lose in an important part of your life, be it your relationship or your job.

However, the use of witty-humor can save your day in such situations.

Witty-humor to the rescue, enables people to reverse their true statement and blanket it with a joke, due to the fear of the worst outcome. This is normally called *"self-defeating use of humor,"* whereby you use humor to build someone else's ego at the expense of your true feeling or opinion.

In order to strategically apply this, the following have to be put into consideration.

- **Be cognitive**

Being cognitive will enable you to find fun in different types of situation. In this case, when you are defending yourself, you can turn a serious situation into a light moment and save yourself.

- **Smile All the Time**

A happy face can save you from serious situations, because humor can be extracted from any situation. This helps you to appear composed and reduces your vulnerability. You can always steer away from conflict through a smile, *as the Joker*.

- **Self-Defeating**

Throw a jab at yourself to show that you are comfortable with yourself. This way, you will draw away the attention from yourself, by showing them you are not interesting and that you are comfortable with your worst deficiencies.

For example, you can get yourself out of trouble by calling yourself the biggest fool on earth. Just saying some thing like that can get you out of trouble.

In case you asked for a salary rise in the middle of a project briefing, just smile and say, *"I'm sorry sir; I am the biggest fool to ask for a salary increment in the middle of a project briefing meeting."*

Yes, it can be ego-deflating, but remember humor and being funny is about putting your ego aside and not to easily emotionally offended as talked about from Chapter 3.

How to Tell Jokes

Now time for some jokes. Rather than give you jokes, let's go over how to tell jokes. *Bah.* Don't be disappointed, would you rather be given a fish or taught how to fish for unlimited fish for life?

Here are key elements for telling jokes:

- **Mind Your Audience**

Always evaluate the kind of audience that you have and read into their moods. You would not want to tell a chemistry joke to a group of accountants. It might fall flat.

You should always consider the mood of your audience. You do not want to crack a joke every other minute to a friend who is not in the mood. You can easily piss them off.

- **Know Your Joke**

The joke is the major content of the delivery. Understanding the basis of the joke enables you to present it with ease.

If it is a joke that you have memorized, you may lose some words but since you understand it, you can still deliver the joke without disclosing it to your audience.

- **Build Anticipation**

The "rule of three" again: *introduction*, *body* and *punch line*. An ideal joke should follow this format. This way, the build-up to the punch line builds up anticipation which is then delivered as a punch line.

For example, Jane is so tall *(introduction)*, that if she needs to take a full body picture *(body)*, it has to come in part 1 & 2 *(punch line)*.

- **Evaluate the Response**

After delivering the punch line, the response of the audience will determine whether to drop that subject or to keep on running with it.

However, do not struggle too much with a joke. Sometimes it is just important to leave the stage on a high note.

Create Your Own Jokes

From talking about how to tell jokes, you have now arrived to its sequel of creating your own jokes that would even make Han Solo crack up at every Chewbacca's *"GRRRWAAAARGGGH!"*

Without further adieu, let's dive right into it without further delay for the Millennium Falcon is not as fast as she's used to and she's not waiting for anybody.

- **Identify the Target Group**

Jokes normally fall under categories. These include jokes about *races*, jokes about *professions*, jokes about *gender*, *baby* jokes and even *religious* jokes. Amongst those, the best target to make a joke about is always **you**. *That's right!* You! *(Take your index-finger right now and point at...you!)* This is because you understand yourself adequately.

Identifying the target of the joke will be the most basic thing you need to do while creating your own joke.

This will give you an idea of the peculiar things that you have always wanted to address.

- **Create the Humor and Relationship**

After identifying the target, you should now close in on the target and identify the exact absurd thing that is of interest to you.

You should now use the formulas that you learned in Chapter 4 about spicing up your conversations. You can use exaggeration, sarcasm or point out the hidden truth.

- **Practice on Delivery**

A good joke can still be poor, if poorly delivered. Timing and how you say it is everything, not just the words. Words alone are meaningless. Remember what they say, *"It's not what you say, but how you say it."* Same thing for jokes.

Mastering delivery requires regular practice and continuous polishing up on the quality of your jokes. This might mean that you rephrase the joke, omit some parts or add new parts until the joke is solid-A.

***

By following the above steps, you can definitely improve on your creative-wit humor and be spontaneous and funny, always coming up with hysterical witty one-liners laughing the wetness out of their eyes.

Your creative-wit requires an incisive approach which can only be developed by regular practice. To assist you in this, here's a weekly training which will guide you through the process of practicing witty-humor.

WEEKLY CREATIVE-WIT TRAINING

DAY I.
- Compliment at least ten people, by using three words and their name.

DAY II.
- Ask at least ten people their opinion about something *(Using 5 words)* and respond to their opinion, building off on what they suggested (*With 5 words*) once and say *"Thanks,"* in order to end the conversation quickly. No more, no less.

DAY III.
- Practice small talk. With your family, or regular people like your vendor. Little random conversations, but keep it going.

DAY IV.
- Repeat DAY I and Day II activities *(But with 5 people per activity)*. For DAY I activity, increase to four words per compliment on each person. DAY II activity,

push the conversation into at least two "5-words" exchanges with each person.

By now, your ability to pick up conversations will be improved. The only remaining thing is to spice up your conversation.

Read about the various things and watch sitcoms. They are the supplies to the most clever witty-lines you can get in this world.

Go step-by-step and by the time you repeat any procedure three or four times, you will have enough idea and practice to start incorporating jokes into your conversations and show off your creative-wit.

***

Being fun and funny most of the times depends on how spontaneous and witty you can allow yourself to be. The points covered throughout this chapter provide a clear guideline on how you can increase your wits and have quick responses to humorous stimuli.

In essence having a quick, sharp and relevant response is a skill that can be worked on to improve your humor delivery mechanisms to be an awesome funny person!

CHAPTER 7

"Now I Got a Funny Story to Tell You..."

Storytelling Comedy

Most people engage in conversations to get to know the other person past their physical appearance. It is important then to ensure that your conversations can depict the correct message and image about yourself.

How would you do this?

A great way of *"marketing"* your personality is through the art of **storytelling**. This puts your audience on the jury's side on things like your intelligence, your ability to memorize, your choice of word and your fluency are judged. Storytelling encompassed them all.

Engaging the imagination of your audience can be perfectly achieved through storytelling. The different emotional rollercoaster presented in stories also provide you, the storyteller, with an opportunity of identifying the preferences of your audience.

For example, while telling a story, you get to notice where they are excited by a certain topic. This will either be shown by their anxiety and total concentration, or by the remorse and emotional concern about the topic of a story. Basically, how emotionally involved and invested they are.

Why storytelling in a conversation?

As the storyteller, you become aware which topics to focus on. Thus, storytelling not only gives you the opportunity to relay your personality, it also provides you with the chance of collecting feedback indirectly from your audience.

Storytelling, just like the other topics already discussed are important ways of making your personality ignite; and with funny stories, you can entertain and make people laugh.

Conversational storytelling also feeds on the spices of a good conversation that talked about previously. They include exaggeration, spontaneity, and metaphors among others.

The Art of Comical Storytelling

Any art, as a technique, can either *be natural* or it can *be natured*. Most of the time, potential natural technique is enhanced so as to increase its effect on humans, whereas poor artistic techniques can be upgraded by training and mentoring and they get natured into perfect skills.

So, question, how do you ensure that that your art of storytelling is enhanced to become interesting and funny?

Answer, by following the guidelines provided below. They will definitely make you realize what you have not been doing, or what you have not been doing adequately.

- **Introduce the Hook**

You cannot just start a story and expect it to be funny. Get the attention of your audience and let them know that a bizarre story is coming. You need to bait the **hook**. *("Hook! Hook! Hook!"* Remember the 1991 Peter Pan's sequel-story movie Hook?)

For example, you can start by saying…"*Let me tell you about a weird thing that happened to me."* You then proceed to, *"While I was coming to school this morning…blah blah blah."* This way, you will have definitely caught the attention of your audience first.

- **Be Natural with the Story**

In essence, do **NOT** try to *be funny*. Yes, don't try hard to be funny. Trying hard to appear funny has always backfired, and you should be able to relate to that trying to impress that hot chick or cute boy.

Try to maintain the story to be as natural as it can be. This way you can maintain the flow of the story without trying too hard to think about the next incident. Trying too hard can be disorienting, which makes you to lose the *oomph*. As a better approach, try to appear to be clueless.

- **Vocabulary**

Use the correct **diction** to describe the appropriate moments. For example, you cannot say that you *"passionately ran"* when the *"dog was chasing you."* Instead, you can say you *"scampered for safety"* at the *"sound of the dog's bark."* This way, you create a humorous actually relatable imagery of a scene with a dog.

Even you can probably picture yourself scampering for safety. The audience relates because they have either seen a person being chased by dogs, or they have been chased by dogs before.

- **The Rule of Three**

Lo and behold, the "rule of three" for the third time again, for third time's the charm. Apply the rule of three into your stories. Remember the **introduction, body,** and ending it with the **punch line.**

Have an **introduction**. For example;

"Last week when I was coming from the airport, I experienced a very embarrassing situation. We shared a taxi with a man who claimed to know me from way back..."

At this point, the listener probably gets the origin of the story. You might not want to dwell on this part because it kills the interest of the story. A brief introduction *hooks* the attention of the listener and readies them for the details in the **body**. For example;

"...so I entered the taxi and this man suddenly turns and calls me by my name. Yeah, he called me by my two names. He said, 'Hi Jane Doe.'"

At this point the curiosity of your listener is definitely off the chains. Go on about how you ignored the person and other few details of the happenings in the taxi, but you could not get out of the taxi and until you reached your destination. At this point, you are building the anticipation of the **climax**.

"As I disembarked from the taxi, this stranger also got out of the taxi. This time even helping the taxi guy to unload my luggage. This guy was driving me nuts. I yelled at him, telling him to stop following me or I will call the police. I was so enraged I attracted a small crowd."

Drop the **punch line**:

"After causing that entire ruckus and as I was getting my phone to call the police, I saw my boyfriend/girlfriend. And guess what? He/she was laughing at me. In that same moment, camera crews emerged from all sorts of directions and John Smith was standing in front of me saying...'WAVE TO THE CAMERA.'"

***

The **above scenario** gives you a whole perspective of how you can create and tell a funny story, especially in the midst of a conversation.

Follow these guides and see how it works for you. *Oh it's MAGIC, you know.*

This can also be applied especially when improvising/developing a story instantly from the conversation **(Topic)** brought about by your audience. You can pick a point out of what your audience has said and turn it into a story, but always ensure that this witty approach maintains the relevance of the existing story.

Create Your Funny Story

Very many funny, weird and embarrassing experiences that you would love to share with other people have occurred in your life. From childhood up to the current age that are. However, you can't wrap it all and tell it out in one moment, you have to categorize everything and place them in different segments.

For you to create your funny story you have to jog your memory and either tell something that happened to you, or something that you vividly remember.

***

Question is, how would you tell out your experiences?

Choose a Topic:

Identify the **topic** that you think has the best experiences that you can recall.

For example if you choose to create a funny story about your life, you can either choose to use your childhood experiences or you can decide to create a story about your most recent experience. As an example, if you choose to tell us about your childhood experience, you can start like this;

"When I was a kid, I could hardly stay a full day without getting into some kind of trouble. This was not because I was naughty but it just somehow happened."

Create the Characters:

A good story should have at least three characters. Too many characters in a story can create a confusion about the facts, which removes the simplicity of the story. You can picture a situation where a short story has fourteen characters, how do you even name them?

In this example, let's create the **characters**. Apart from you, there is your best friend, there is the teacher, and then there is the roadside vendor.

After identifying the characters in your story, you have to create the connection between the characters. How do you create the connection between your characters in your story?

Hold your horses! That's the next point.

Make the Plot and Setting:

The best way of creating a *connection* between your characters is by placing them in a **setting**. You can achieve a perfect setting by creating a **plot**. Identify the plot, choose the setting and the characters in it.

In our example, let us select the setting to be at the entrance of the school premises.

So far, we have the characters and the setting. *We need the plot.* Let's talk about the naughty kids who steal from the roadside vendor.

Be Descriptive:

Pay attention to **details**. As much as you prune your story to avoid unnecessary details, you should ensure that the *main setting* and the *main characters* are adequately described.

This description should be detailed in a manner that it can create an image in the minds of your listeners. In your description, include the color, shape and size of grotesque features.

For example, let us describe the scene, which is the entrance to the school compound.

"I waited for my friends at the school's entrance. The worn tarmac pavement were full of brown and yellow leaves. The site of bushy flower beds and lawns made it look quite

unkempt. Across the road, a fruit vendor was washing apples which appeared to be very juicy. I could see the school bus coming at what I considered to be a snail's pace..."

Describe the Characters:

Notice the in-depth rich characterizations of the characters for you to be able to get an idea to who they are:

"Gustavo, the fruit vendor was an old man who always wore a white apron. Today he looked a little bit disturbed. His trademark round hat was missing..."

"One-by-one, my friends alighted from the school bus. Ezra, the red-haired good ole lad from Ireland was carrying a green backpack that had a water bottle on the side. One of his shoe laces was dangling, and he appeared very pissed with the new haircut that he was spotting..."

"Chong followed him out of the bus. You would always assume that he was smiling at you. His large teeth were out, as always, and he was carrying a few books on his hands."

"Krishna on the other hand, the oldest and biggest appeared from behind the bus. According to what I learned later on, he had used the back window of the bus as his exit."

Link the Characters to the Plot:

While creating your own funny stories, ensure that your descriptions contain a bit of exaggerations as to make it spicy *(but not necessary hot needed)*.

As an **exercise,** try linking up the scene with the characters and end up with a funny story.

In any story, there is always a conflict involving the **protagonist** and the **antagonist,** in essence, the *good guy* versus the *bad guy*.

Ever notice how bad guys in stories and movies always have more fun and appear more cool and interesting? So in this example, you can let you and your friends be the bad guys.

Give someone your story and look at their reaction. Follow the steps below in order to come up with a funny story of your own:

- Strategize/Plan.

- Identify the characters and plot.

- Chose the setting of the story.

- Create the connection between the characters and the scene.

- Create a conclusion.

- Edit your story and tie loose ends.

- Offer it to another person for criticism.

- Take the critics positively and polish your story until it can be humorous.

***

In order to have an awesome to tell, continue crafting the whole process over and again.

Follow these steps, and you should be able to create your own funny stories and present them in your conversation to another person reassessing how they react then tweak your story next time.

That is how you will monitor your progress and improve your storytelling skill. Don't quit.

CHAPTER 8

"I Like You...You're Funny!"

Apply Humor in Everyday Life

The ability to see the humor in your everyday life actually requires a very open (receptive) mind. Deriving humor from little things such as how people walk and other general incidents requires a creative mind that supersedes logical thinking.

Seeing humor in everyday life is not just about laughing. It is about the ability to interpret ordinary things and create your own version which extends past the visual portrayal of the naked eye.

Humor is a key determinant in a person's happiness. Having a sense of humor increases a person's happiness while lacking a sense of humor, decreases the likelihood of someone to be happy.

By being receptive to different stimuli, we can derive humor from almost every aspect of life and improve our well being. The benefits of happiness in your life include:

- Mental stability

- Reduction in stress and blood pressure

- Improved interaction with family, colleagues and friends

- Increased ability to solve conflicts

See the Funny in Everything

So, how do you leverage on everyday activities so as to derive humor and the benefit from being happy? The following procedure will guide you through the process of deriving humor in everyday activities.

- Always **reflect** about what it would mean to have a humorous outlook on normal everyday happenings. Try to understand what it means to be having a humorous and happy life. For example, do not always look at how tough ties have become. Get some time off the financial and work related issues and fantasize; this increases your ability to be imaginative and creative, making you to see the possible existence of a happy side of life.

- **Identify** areas where other people derive their humor from. Try to identify about five things that might be funny and relate to them passively. Set a goal for yourself to personally identify at least 3-5 funny things for one week. You won't miss them. They are all over, just observe the way life rolls, and you will identify them. For example, warning signs can be funny, if you look at them in a funny manner. Some headlines are also catchy and very funny too. Take your time and look at different things, and you will identify the fun possibilities that are already existent.

- Watch **sitcoms** and **comedies,** and also read **funny articles**. This can help you to understand the delivery techniques of humorous statements. For example, you can learn so much about banter and sarcasm by watching sitcoms.

- Learn to *have conversions* in **short sentences**. This ensures that you reduce your chances of being boring, as long as you converse through open-ended questions. Also make sure that your conversations do not sound like an interview.

- **SMILE.** Always smile. This way, you attract people toward you, instead of you having to always be the one to start conversations; other people can easily start conversations with you too. By seeing the warm side that you portray, you become likable and funny by default.

- **Be cheerful.** By being cheerful, you are most likely to emit positive vibes from your inner self. You can dance at a party, you can make faces and you can generally draw happy and funny characters in your life. Always be cheerful, it helps a lot.

Train Your Brain Right

Your brain is the most powerful tool that your human body possesses. It influences decisions, attitude and emotions. These are the necessary components for building your imaginative capacity which is all the facility that you require to build up your humor.

But how do you train your brain to be able to facilitate your humor capacity?

This can be done by *engaging in activities* which increase your **right-side of the brain.**

The left-brain, right brain dominance theory identifies the *"right-brain"* is associated with **creativity** and **innovation**, while the *"left-brain"* is associated with **logic.**

Training your brain to see the humor in everyday's life will therefore activate your creativity and boost your intuition, emotions, music, reading, color recognition, images recognition and playfulness of yourself.

- **Exercise**

By engaging in **physical activity,** the body gets to improve the condition of the brain with respect to its functioning. Body workout has an impact on brain functioning because it helps in the stimulation of the growth of the brain cells.

Physical exercise, especially *aerobic exercises*, is known to cause an increase in the heart rate, enabling sufficient supply of oxygen into the brain. This can help in boosting your **memory capacity**.

Exercising also assists in **relaxation**, which is important for ensuring that you can regulate your breathing, which is very helpful in boosting your self-confidence.

- **Diets and Nutrition**

Brains require frequent *nourishment*; hence, replenishment can be accomplished by using **nutrients**. Foods that are rich in antioxidants and vitamins are helpful in boosting comprehension and cognition. The necessary nutrients can be gotten from eating foods like whole grains, nuts, vegetables, fish and fruits.

Breakfast is said to be the most important meal of the day. By including the foods mentioned above in your breakfast, and especially proteins, you can be guaranteed of a more energetic and cognitive day ahead of you.

That is what is required in order to be humorous and funny.

- **Alternate Your Schedule**

Maintaining routines is boring. **Shake up** your routines so as to improve your brain functionality. This is a practical way of training your brain in a way that increases your creative space and get new perspectives and experience new happenings.

How do you shake up your routine?

You can shake up your routine by changing your eating spot, eating habits, your recreation areas, dressing, travelling, books you read and the items that you watch or listen to.

This diversity can be instrumental in highlighting the different functionalities of the brain that are best identified by the left-brain, right-brain dominance theory.

- **Reduce TV Time**

Too much television *increases* **brain idleness** and encourages **brain inactivity**. This is not what you need for the purposes of developing your likelihood of identifying and applying humor in everyday life.

Reduce the time you spend watching the television by increasing your outdoor activities like walking, visiting friends and also by reading funny novels, journals and newspapers. Anything that keeps the brain active and engaged.

- **Put Your Brain to Test**

Engage your brain to rigorous and random tests that will ensure it is subjected to unstructured responses.

These include debates with your friends, learning new languages and cultures, trying out puzzles and, *once in a while*, you should also multitask.

These enable your brain synapses to be active and adaptive to new environments, which is very important in applying humor in everyday life. These activities assist the brain to become cognitive, thus, helping you to identify humor in everyday life and activities.

- **Beat Logic**

Logic has its necessary place, but it is very important to reason beyond logic for you to be able to identify humor in everyday life. Look beyond the obvious. Look past the message and you will find fun and humor in everything that happens in your everyday life.

For example, *why is it a zebra crossing when it is humans who use it?*

Just beat the logic, and you will find the humor in the previous statement.

<u>*Gosh...*You're Damn Funny as Hell</u>!
<u>*Stop Making Me Laugh!*</u> :D

Being funny and possessing a sense of humor are assets to your existence.

Firstly, this is because of the various stand-alone benefits that come from being humorous alone. They include mirth and laughter, which are responsible for; enhancing your conversation and interaction ability with other people, reducing your stress levels through tension release, and as well as helpful in the diffusing of difficult and uncomfortable situations.

It is also noteworthy to clear out a misconception about being funny. It does not necessarily mean you have to be a stand-up comedian, or become king of comedy. That is because you never have to be a comedian to be funny.

However, not every person is born with the charm to be witty, funny and humorous. Most people pick it up along the way as they grow, but some have to learn and train their brain in a manner that will make them funny, humorous and witty.

Just to be clear, this does not make the ones who have to learn the techniques any less funny or humorous. Like it is normally said, "*The end justifies the means.*"

The bearer of the benefits of being funny will be you. So soldier on and work on improving on your ability to be funny and likable.

What you have now is a clear guidance on how to improve your interpersonal relationship with other people by improving your sense of humor. Having a sense of humor will ensure that you posses the ability to identify humor and also the ability to develop humor; hence fun.

You have now been given all the ingredients and directions of enhancing your sense of humor. You now understand that it is not necessary to become funny, but, however, you can be fun. You now have the ability to identify with the lighter side of life. You can now comfortably develop your own fun personality, and cultivate your unique and relatable sense of humor.

So what are you waiting for? Go out there and have fun. Go out there and be fun. Go out there and be an inspiration to other people who are having a hard time because of their inability to be fun, funny or humorous. Help them join "the movement" of sharing love and laughter.

Go out and help to make this world a happy place. **HAVE FUN.**

Be FUNNY or DIE!

Printed in Great Britain
by Amazon